# SAMVEDA IN A NUTSHELL

## DR. JAGADEESH PILLAI

Made with ❤ on the Notion Press Platform
www.notionpress.com

!! Dedicated to all wisdom seekers !!

# Contents

# Contents

# Prayer

Om Asato Maa Sad-Gamaya |

Tamaso Maa Jyotir-Gamaya |

Mrtyor-Maa Amrtam Gamaya |

Om Shaantih Shaantih Shaantih ||

Meaning:

Lead us from the unreal to the real

Lead us from darkness to light

Lead us from death to immortality

Aum peace, peace, peace!

❧❧❧

# About The Author

**Dr. Jagadeesh Pillai** four times Guinness World Record holder, a voracious reader, writer, and true research scholar was born in Varanasi, the abode of Lord Shiva. He is Ph.D. in Vedic Science. He is a multi-faceted polymath with innate qualities, creative ideas and many remarkable achievements. Although his roots extend back to "Gods own Country"(Kerala), the residents of Varanasi feel proud of him and adore him as a child of Varanasi who caters to every individual in need without any expectations. A deep study into his profile reflects that he has added so many feathers to his cap which makes him quite unique. He is a four times Guinness Book of World Records Holder in the following subjects :

1.  "Script to Screen" which he achieved by producing and directing a state of art animation film within the shortest time possible by breaking the earlier set record by Canadians. There are many national and international Awards and Recognitions to his credit.

2.  Longest Line of Post Cards which he has done on the occasion of 163 years of Indian Postal Day by 16300 post cards. The event was also connected with a questionnaire about Indian Flag.

3.  Largest Poster Awareness Campaign – This was achieved by designing an awareness campaign on the subject "Beti Bachao – Beti Padhao".

4.  Largest Envelop – Towards tribute to Prime Minister's initiative 'Make in India' – he has created about 4000 sq meter envelop using waste papers.

5.  Attempted by lighting 70000 candles on a 210 kg cake to celebrate the 70th Indian Independence day recorded in World Records India.

6.  Attempted a documentary on Dhamek Stupa of Sarnath dubbing in 17 languages, result is waiting from Guinness World Records.

He is versatile in Gita teaching. The young generation is fond of his Gita teaching and he has changed the life of many young through his continued motivational boost up and teachings.

He has composed and sung Gayatri Mantra in 1008 different tunes.

He has composed and sung Hanuman Chalisa in 108 different tunes.

He has composed and sung hundreds of Sanskrit Bhajans, Patriotic songs, etc.

He has written and directed so many short films and documentaries for awareness campaigns.

He has done voluntary services to UP Police and Kerala Police to spread awareness campaigns on the various issue through videos and photography.

He is on the path of authoring thousands of books on Indian culture, Indian Temples, and the life of extraordinary people.

It is hard to believe that he has produced and directed more than 100 Documentaries on a particular city (Varanasi) which is done by a single person.

He has helped and guided more than 25 boys and girls to achieve world records through various creative and innovative methods.

A multifaceted person who can apply the best of his intellect using the God-given blessings which have been showered upon every human being granting them an immense capacity to learn, experience, and experiment with many things and do wonders in this world of discrimination and disparities.

He is a teacher and a student at the same time who always learns every day and teaches every day. As a master, his weakness was that he never sticks to a particular subject. Perhaps this weakness gives him the strength to master any area which he came across.

Each of his days dawned with learning a new topic and he spend most of his time experimenting and researching it.

He is also a selfless social activist and a motivational speaker.

His life was full of struggle, ups and downs, and failures.

But he never gave up and faced all his trials and tribulations full of confidence. Today he is a successful young man with a lot of enthusiasm and rich life experience.

He has sung full Ram Charita Manas 51 hours audio by his own composition. He has also sung the whole Bhagavad-Gita in his own composition with a rhythmic background.

He has also sung "Lokah Samastha Sukhino Bhavantu" in 50 different languages.

Currently working on a detailed and scientific study on Veda, Upanishad, Puranas, Bhagavad Gita, etc.

He has composed and sung Hanuman Chalisa in 108 different compositions and Gayatri Mantra in 1008 different compositions.

<u>Awards</u>

Four Times Guinness World Records

Winner of Mahatma Gandhi Vishwa Shanti Puraskar

Mahatma Gandhi Global Peace Ambassador

Kashi Ratna Award

Dr. APJ Abdul Kalam Motivational Person of the Year 2017

Mother Teresa Award

Indira Gandhi Priyadarshini Award

Bharat Vikas Ratna Award

Udyog Ratna Award

Vigyan Prasar Award

Poorvanchal Ratn Samman

# Preface

The Samaveda is an ancient collection of Vedic Sanskrit hymns, which date back to late 2nd millennium BCE. It is the oldest existing Veda and consists of 1,549 verses. The Samaveda follows a metre that is different from other Vedas; it has 32 melodious chants that were composed over two thousand years ago by Lalita Vistara. These melodic chants are believed to have been used as part of ritual sacrifices in Hindu temples and homes. The contents of the Samveda consist of a variety of topics such as philosophy, knowledge, Dharma, devotion to gods and goddesses, Yajna (ritual fire sacrifice), worship rituals for arati or puja (worship) for various gods and goddesses , descriptions about 'Upanishads' (mystic secrets) , social conduct, various medicinal plants etc. It is generally seen as a sourcebook for Indian philosophy, cultural values and ideas about our cosmos.

This book offers a clear and concise understanding of the Samaveda, its verses, and the wisdom they impart. It is an invaluable resource for anyone looking to gain insight into this ancient text and its teachings. By delving into the Samveda, readers can gain a deeper appreciation of the spiritual and philosophical foundations of Hinduism and its enduring relevance to modern life.

# Introduction to Samveda

Samaved is one of the four canonical texts of Hinduism, which is traditionally recited to honor the Hindu god Shri Vishnu. The text was composed by Maharishi Veda Vyasa, who authored all of the four Vedas.

The text is divided into two khandas, each containing 75 short chapters. The first Khanda, or 'book', is known as the Deva Khanda, which consists of hymns dedicated to various deities. This section contains various hymns of praise, such as hymns dedicated to Indra, Agni, Rudra, Ushas, Varun and Bhaga. The hymns of the Deva Khanda are meant to honor and invoke the gods to bestow their blessings upon the worshipper.

The second khanda, the Aranyaka Khanda, is composed of hymns dedicated to various rituals and ceremonies. This section contains various hymns related to sacred offerings such as soma offerings, pouring ghee into sacred fires and making offerings of clarified butter.

The content of Samaveda focuses primarily on rituals and

ceremonies of yore, focusing on the knowledge of rituals and their meaning to the worshipper. It covers topics related to the science of music, the purpose and meaning of fasting, the importance of austerities, and how rituals and ceremonies were conducted thousands of years ago.

The language of Samaveda is also unique. It is composed in two different languages, Sanskrit and Prakrit. The Vedic chants which feature in the hymns are composed in Sanskrit, while the commentary and mantras which accompany the hymns are composed in Prakrit.

Samaveda helps to bring together all the different aspects of Hindu life and from this single source Hindus can have access to their most important Vedic texts. It is part of the core scriptures for adherents of Hinduism, a religion which has been passed down through the generations for thousands of years and continues to be a major source of learning for many today.

The teachings found in Samaveda are still relevant today and provide spiritual sustenance and guidance for millions of Hindus throughout the world. By offering this guidance, it helps Dharma to continue its cycle of existence. Samaveda is therefore an invaluable portion of the Hindu Vedas and its teachings should be taken seriously by those who are seeking to enrich their spiritual experience.

# CHAPTER TWO

# RISHIES OF SAMVED

The Rishies of Samved are an ancient Hindu religious practice, believed to have originated in Vedic times. It is a form of traditional Hindu worship and devotion centered around specific rituals and activities, and is said to have been revealed by the Aak guru, "Veda-Vyasa", in the Samveda.

Rishies of Samved involve the worship of various gods and goddesses, and many of the spiritual practices that may be found in Hinduism. It is believed that the rishies are able to access nonphysical realms and source divine knowledge and inner wisdom from the gods.

The focal point of Rishies of Samved is the chanting of hymns in which various gods are invoked: the rishies who practice the rituals often chant mantras over Sanskrit script on which the hymns to be chanted are inscribed. This enables the rishies to communicate with the deities, requesting their blessings and guidance, and to meditate on their divine wisdom.

The ritual of worshipping includes several steps, beginning with an invocation to the deities, followed by the chanting of hymns and, then, the recital of prayers. During the recital, flowers, incense, and other offerings, such as fruit, may be presented to the gods. Following this, the rishies close off their prayers with different types of emotional and spiritual exercises, such as offerings of thanksgiving and expressions of renewal. This is completed with a benediction, or final prayer, to bring the ritual to a close.

Rishies of Samved also have a rich and detailed mythology that is deeply ingrained in their religious beliefs and practices. One such myth explains why the gods are invoked so regularly in their chants and rituals – the gods and goddesses provide protection and guidance, and they act as a bridge to the physical and spiritual realms.

Not only is Rishies of Samved an important part of Hinduism, but its practices have flourished beyond the Hindu faith. The practices and rituals of Rishies of Samved have become adapted and adopted in many parts of the world, with spiritual seekers seeking to take part in the rituals for personal growth and transformation.

In conclusion, Rishies of Samved is a significant and rich religious practice, with roots in Hinduism and growing beyond its traditional boundaries. Its rituals and practices provide spiritual seekers with the means to communicate with the gods for guidance and protection. In following the practice of Rishies of Samved, individuals gain access to nonphysical realms and divine knowledge, as well as find solace and strength to navigate through challenging times.

# CHAPTER THREE

In Hindu mythology, the devas of the Samaveda are deities who are believed to be in charge of protecting and organizing the world. The devas of the Samaveda are said to come from the eight Vedic gods, who were associated with various aspects of the universe. The Samaveda is one of the four Vedas, the most ancient scriptures of Hinduism and is traditionally attributed to the sage Vyasadeva.

The devas of the Samaveda are closely associated with Indra, the Vedic god of thunder and king of the gods. They are believed to act as Indra's attendants and guardians of the laws of nature, as well as to work closely with humans in their daily spiritual and material endeavors.

The Samaveda is composed of verses that describe the duties of the devas, as well as their different powers and capabilities. Each deva is responsible for a specific area of the cosmos, from the elements to the planets and stars. The devas are believed to be able to influence the forces of the universe, to bring about both good and bad outcomes.

The devas of the Samaveda are also seen as the spiritual representatives of nature in Hinduism. This is best shown in their role as wanderers in the material world, which constrains them to the tasks of creating and protecting the universe, providing material blessings, and resolving conflicts between humans.

The Samaveda is filled with references to devas, stating that they are responsible for protecting and creating the universe as well as maintaining an unending cycle of existence. Devas are also described as messengers of the gods, able to connect earthly and spiritual realms.

The devas of the Samaveda are also connected to various aspects of the material world. They are believed to be responsible for protecting humans from evil forces, ensuring the sun, moon and stars shine, and for the growth and sustenance of plants and animals.

In closing, the devas of the Samaveda serve an essential role in Hinduism, providing a physical and spiritual representation of the forces of nature, enabling humans to interact and communicate with the other realms of existence. The Samaveda provides a great foundation for further exploration of this important aspect of Hindu thought.

# CHAPTER FOUR

# VERSES OF SAMVEDA

The Vedas are the foundation of the Hindu faith, and are among the most ancient religious texts in the world. Samveda is one of the four Vedic scriptures, and is composed of hymns and verses prayerfully recited to invoke the benevolence of the gods. A key component of the Hindu way of life, Vedic verses have been studied and savored since the dawn of civilization.

There are two thousand verses in Samveda, some of which are among the oldest, most sacred, and highly revered Hindu texts. The verses are composed of mantras and hymns, as well as invocations to the gods and goddesses. They range from prayers for good health and prosperity to esoteric explorations of the cosmic forces. There are verses about the power of faith, and about transcending the physical realm and returning to the source of all existence. Each verse contains deep philosophical and spiritual revelations, offering guidance and insight into the inner workings of the cosmos.

The Samveda verses form a beautiful tapestry of

knowledge, wisdom, and spiritual truth. They are rich in symbolism, symbolism which reveals the interconnectedness of all things. For example, a popular Samveda mantra explains that "everything is one, and everything is united", and "everything is part of something bigger". Through these verses, Hindus are encouraged to recognize and appreciate the nuances of diversity.

Interestingly, the Samveda verses contain many healing and medicinal properties. Hindus believe that the recitation of these verses has a calming effect, providing the listener with physical and mental rejuvenation. The Sanskrit language used in the verses is believed to be especially potent, namely because of its rich and deep roots in ancient Hindu culture.

Finally, it is said that Samveda verses have immense power in terms of manifesting one's desires. When chanted with faith and sincerity, believers claim that individuals are able to attract good fortune, abundance, and success into their lives.

The wonders of the Samveda can never truly be fully comprehended. With ancient wisdom contained in its verses, it is a text which provides solace, healing, and guidance to Hindus across the globe. It is a timeless reminder of the power of faith and the interconnectedness of the cosmos.

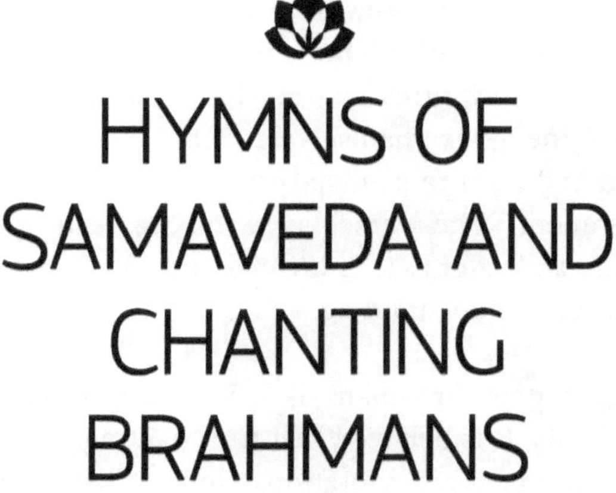

# CHAPTER FIVE

# HYMNS OF SAMAVEDA AND CHANTING BRAHMANS

Hymns, verses of Samved, and chanting Brahmans have been an integral part of Indian culture since ancient times. Samved, being the oldest religious text of the Rig Veda form an integral part of Hindu Religious practice. Chanting Brahmans can generally be seen in any Hindu temple.

Hymns are the words or verses sung to praise the gods and goddesses of their culture. It is believed that these are the actual words of the gods and goddesses that have been passed down to the people through oral tradition. These hymns are often taken from the ancient texts like Rig Veda, Yajurveda, and Samveda. The hymns are chanted to invoke the blessings of the gods and to express the emotions of devotion and joy. The various hymns have meanings that are significant and are a tribute to the spiritual power that is believed to be within them.

The verses of Samveda otherwise called as Mantras have a more profound meaning and purpose. They are chanted as prayers and meditations to gain the inner peace and the pleasure of the divinity. The verses are the most sacred of all the Vedic scriptures and are believed to be theactual words of the gods themselves. They are chanted with devotion and faith to gain spiritual guidance, comfort and enlightenment. The verses of Samveda also symbolize prosperity and valor as they are chanted with full reverence and profound understanding.

The chanting of Brahmans is a very important part of Hindu rituals. It is believed that the chanting of Brahmans invokes the positive vibrations and is believed to be responsible for removing negative energies and achieving the desired results. The chanting and prayers are usually done by a group of priests who are clad in white and sit in a triangular form. These priests chant continuously for hours in order to establish a connection between the devotees and the divine.

Hymns, verses of Samved, and chanting of Brahmans are a part of Indian culture for centuries. They are a source of spiritual encouragement and have a deep significance in attaining inner peace. All throughout India, these components of Hindu culture are practiced with reverence and joy, and the devotees gain satisfaction from the divine connection.

# CHAPTER SIX

# INDIAN CLASSICAL MUSIC AND SAMVEDA

Indian classical music, also known as "shastriya sangeet" is an ancient form of music, in existence for at least 2500 years. It is linked to religious texts and traditions and is used for many purposes other than entertainment such as the narration of religious stories, the facilitation of trained musicians for the continuation of religious activities and for the promotion of emotional and physical well-being. It is believed to be connected to the Vedas, a set of ancient Indian scriptures, and in particular to the Samaveda, one of its four components.

The Samaveda is an important part of Indian culture as it contains many of its significant religious texts. It discusses Vedic rituals, worships, chants, mantras and music. Also, several simple and complicated notes are discussed which form the basis of Indian classical music. Vedic music was used to accompany certain religious services such as the performance of yajnas, a kind of sacrifice, fire rituals and war rituals. This indicates a close tie and influence of the Samaveda in Indian classical music and the performance of raga.

The Samaveda is believed to be one of the oldest known examples of music notation. According to some scholars, the Samaveda was the first to use the system of recording music in notation. It provides an amalgamation of diverse styles of music from diverse cultures and backgrounds, with an emphasis on simplicity, so that anyone could learn and perform music from it. This collection of notes and styles played a huge role in charting the development of ancient Indian music.

The melody and tonal system of Indian classical music is believed to be modelled after the hymns of the Samaveda. The concept of the raga and the tonal system used in Indian classical music can be found in the Samaveda. The way ragas were conceived and developed is studied in the Samaveda, making it an important source of Indian musical knowledge. Additionally, many of the intricacies of the rhythmic vocal gymnastics and the intricate note combinations, that are found in traditional Indian ragas, also originate from the Samaveda.

In conclusion, it is undeniable that the Samaveda had a huge influence on the development of Indian classical music. The Samaveda is both an important source of music as well as an influential source of knowledge for musicians wishing to explore the depth of Indian classical music. The intricate note combinations and tonality, rhythm and melody found in traditional Indian ragas, directly stem from the Samaveda. To understand the true potential and evolution of Indian classical music, it is imperative to understand the connection and relation between music and the Samaveda.

# CHAPTER SEVEN

# SAMAVEDA AND UPANISHADS

The Samaveda is one of the four Vedas and is a collection of hymns and mantras. While all four Vedas are considered a part of Hinduism, the Samaveda has a special place in that it holds an intimate connection to the Upanishads, the primary source of non-dualist Hindu philosophy. This connection is seen in both the language of the Samaveda and the content of the Upanishadic texts.

One of the aspects that binds the Samaveda and the Upanishads is their mutual reliance on the Vedic language. This language is drawn from the Indo-European root, and has its roots in the Rigveda. While the language of the Rigveda is primarily religious in nature, the language of the Samaveda has a more profound philosophical essence. It is this language that is used in the Upanishads to explore and explain the various aspects of Atman, Brahman and the other essential principles of Hinduism. In this sense, it is the language of the Samaveda that truly binds the two texts.

The content of the Upanishads is also related to the Samaveda. The teachings of the Samaveda focus primarily on the idea of moksha, the path to liberation. The principles of the Samaveda are found in the Upanishads, which follow the same path towards moksha. Through the continual repetition of the mantras, it is hoped that the seeker will ultimately attain enlightenment and experience the truth of Brahman. The philosophy and language of the Samaveda thus lay the foundation for the Upanishadic thought.

The teachings of the Samaveda and the Upanishads thus combine to provide a comprehensive understanding of the essential concepts of Hinduism. While the Samaveda focuses on the mantras that serve as a guide to liberation, the Upanishads discuss the philosophy and greater principles such as Atman and Brahman. Together, the Samaveda and the Upanishads provide a core framework for non-dualist Hinduism that is essential for any seeker seeking to attain the truth of Atman and Brahman.

The close bond between the Samaveda and the Upanishads is thus evident. Through the use of the Vedic language, the Samaveda forms a connection to the language of the Upanishads that binds the two texts together. At the same time, the Samaveda also provides a philosophy and content that form the major principles of the Upanishads. This close connection between the Samaveda and the Upanishads thus forms a core foundation for the non-dualist Hinduism.

# SAMVEDA AND BHAGAVAD GITA

The Samveda, one of the four main texts of the Vedas, is a collection of hymns that extol the glory of God and His virtues. It is considered to be the earliest text in Indian tradition and has had a profound influence on Hindu thought and practice in the millennia that followed. One of the most significant connections between the Samveda and the Bhagavad Gita is the concept of Ishvara, which is found in both texts.

The Samveda is the source of many of the ideas and themes that are explored in the Bhagavad Gita. In the Samveda, Ishvara is presented as a personal god who is the source of the universe and is responsible for creating and sustaining the world. In the Bhagavad Gita, Ishvara is presented as a form of God that is both omniscient and omnipresent. In other words, Ishvara is a representation of an all-powerful, all-knowing, and all-pervading divine power.

The Samveda also highlights the importance of devotion to Ishvara, which is also a key concept in the Bhagavad Gita. The Samveda emphasizes that one's spiritual journey should involve a deep relationship with God that is expressed through love and devotion. This devotion is manifested through one's thoughts, words, and actions, and is seen as a way to harmonize with the universal divine power. Similarly, it is through devotion to Ishvara that one can attain moksha, or liberation, in the Bhagavad Gita.

The Samveda and the Bhagavad Gita also share the concept of karma, which is the law of cause and effect. In the Samveda, karma is seen as a way of attaining moksha, in which one's actions are determined by previous actions and their consequences. These actions create an endless cycle of cause and effect that can be broken once one has attained moksha. In the Bhagavad Gita, Arjuna is instructed to act without attachment and to perform duties without expecting results. In other words, he is instructed to act based on one's dharma, or duty. In this way, karma is seen as a way of freeing oneself from the cycle of birth and death.

The Samveda and the Bhagavad Gita also agree on the idea of "sanyasa," or renunciation of material goods and pursuits. In the Samveda, this is seen as a way of achieving moksha, or liberation from the cycle of birth and death. Similarly, in the Bhagavad Gita, Arjuna is instructed to renounce material attachments and instead focus on the divine Self that resides within each individual.

# CHAPTER NINE

# SAMAVEDA AND PURANAS

Vedas are a set of scriptures that contain ancient religious and spiritual knowledge, written in Sanskrit and dated back to nearly 1500 BCE. The Samaveda is one of the four Vedas and it primarily consists of mantras and melodies for the performance of Vedic rituals. It is also known as the Veda of chants, as it contains purely text of various hymns from the Rig-Veda.

The eighteen Puranas are a group of ancient texts believed to have been written between 400 BCE and 1100 CE. These religious texts provide an exhaustive account of Hinduism and its history, rituals and beliefs. They contain stories, archetypes, and legends, which are often used to illustrate principles of morality and to suggest the path of dharmic life.

The connection between Samaveda and the eighteen Puranas is strong, especially in terms of the use of mythic and legendary stories to carry religious and spiritual messages. Both scriptures contain stories and diagrams, many of which have the same purpose. For example, the

Panchavinshati of Samaveda and the Devipurana of Puranas both contain descriptions of the origin and symbolism of the five indriyas and the six ayatanas or sense organs. In both scriptures, stories are used to illustrate principles of morality and dharma, such as sacrificial and filial duties, as well as other moral codes.

The Samaveda and the Puranas are also connected in terms of their form and content. The Puranas are said to be a unique, comprehensive and corrective form of the Vedas and the Vedic culture. In other words, they enable us to understand the Vedic duties and culture, to a great extent. The Samveda, which is said to be the Veda of chants, is also linked to the Puranas as chants and hymns from the Rig-Veda play a prominent role in the Puranas.

The connection between Samveda and the eighteen Puranas can also be seen in terms of their respective characters. Characters from Samveda such as Indra, Vayu, Maheshwara, Rudra, Agni, etc. have their counterparts in the Puranas such as Vishnu, Surya, Brahma, Varuna, etc. Hence, a study of the Samaveda and the Puranas can be very beneficial as it helps to understand the relationship between characters in both texts.

Overall, the connection between Samaveda and the Puranas is strong. Both scriptures contain stories, archetypes, and legends, which are used to illustrate principles of morality, dharma and religion. Additionally, both scriptures make use of the same characters and the same forms of narration. Therefore, a study of both scriptures can yield valuable insight into the ancient history, culture, and beliefs of Hinduism.

# SAMVEDA AND FIVE ELEMENTS

The Rigveda, Sama Veda and Yajur Veda are considered to be the oldest and most essential sacred texts of Hinduism. Samaveda, in particular, is a collection of chants and hymns taken from the Rigveda that are still used in ancient Hindu rituals today. Although often overlooked, these sacred texts of Samaveda contain significant information regarding the ancient Hindu belief in the five elements which make up all of creation.

The Samaveda consists of chants and hymns dedicated to different Hindu gods and these can be used as an allegorical metaphor for the five elements. Each element is a fundamental part of what makes up creation, and through Samaveda, Hinduism believes these elements are brought together in harmonious balance.

The first element is earth, or prithvi. This element is symbolized by the food that is offered to the gods during Hindu ceremonies. Additionally, the ritualistic chanting of the Samaveda is thought to create vibrations that bring this element into the physical world.

The second element is water, or jal. Water is a symbol of life and is said to be the nourisher of the Earth. It is this element which helps to bring life to physical things and contains the potential for growth. In Samaveda, water is symbolically represented by the chanting of the hymns that invoke deities such as Agni, Vishnu, and Soma.

The third element is fire, or agni. Fire is thought to be the source of transformation and empowerment of the elements. In Samaveda, the fire representing this element is literally ablaze during rituals and chanting is used to invoke its unifying power.

The fourth element is wind, or Vayu. Wind is a symbol of movement and change and is often associated with divine forces and storms. In Samaveda, the wind is invoked through the recitation of hymns.

The fifth element is ether, or akasha. Ether is believed to be the source of creation, containing pure potential and containing the knowledge of past and present. In Samaveda, this element is often times symbolized by the temple venue of the ceremony itself which provides the backdrop for the chanting.

Together, the five elements of creation are brought into harmony through the chanting of the Samaveda. This harmony helps create a harmonious environment for the gods to manifest and bless those present. The rituals of the Samaveda remind us that balance is the key to harmony and education. Through understanding the five elements and how they work together in harmony, we can gain a deeper understanding of the universe and our place in it.

# CHAPTER ELEVEN

# SINGING AND CHANTING STYLE OF SAMVEDA MANTRAS

The Samaveda is the third of the universally accepted four Vedas, revered by Hindus as the most sacred and ancient of all Hindu texts. The Samaveda is one of the most musically vibrant scriptures to have come out of the Indian subcontinent. While Vedic ritual is said to grant humans certain benefits, it is also hypothesized that the chanting of the mantras of the Samaveda is a way of connecting with the divine and conveying prayers.

The Samaveda is composed of hymns and chants set to music. Those who chant the Samaveda are known in India as Samaganais. Samaganais use a particular style of singing, distinct from that of the other three Vedas. This style is known as 'Sama Veda Gamaka', and it consists of a complex combination of rhythm, melody and expression that is said to provide a unique experience of spiritual union with the divine.

The particular singing style of the Samaveda enables a direct connection between the chanter and the divine. Samaganais use their voices to create a unique sonic environment, which is said to be a powerful vehicle for chanting important mantras and connecting with the divine. The chants of the Samaveda are not only rooted in ancient Indian culture, but also indebted to music of other cultures. Within the Samaveda, there are various musical forms, such as shlokas, antaras, pavana, viloma and chant styles, which all serve to enhance the spiritual experience of the chanter.

The primary purpose of a Samaganais is to use his/her voice and singing style as a way to directly mediate with the divine. The Samaveda energies and mantras are channeled through the chanting of the Samaganais, creating a powerful sonic atmosphere that has the potential to directly connect the chanter with the divine. Samaganais must learn the unique style of Singing Samveda Vedeka, which is the key element in connecting with the divine. The structure and the tone of voice used in the chanting of the Samaveda are said to be the key to unlocking the magical power of the Samaveda mantras.

Ultimately, the Samaveda is an ancient tradition deeply rooted in Indian culture. It is a spiritual practice that uses a unique and highly sophisticated form of singing and chanting to convey powerful mantras and energies associated with each of the four Vedas. It is a spiritual tradition that speaks to the soul, providing reconnection and insight into the teachings of the Vedas, and bridging the gap between humans and the divine.

# CHAPTER TWELVE

# SAMAVEDA COMMENTARIES BY INTERNATIONAL AUTHORS

Samveda is an ancient Indian spiritual text, which is an important part of the Vedic tradition that serves as a source of knowledge and wisdom. It is one of the four Vedas and is often called the "kerosene of the Vedas". Samveda is traditionally viewed as the secret form of Vedic chanting, featuring subtle passages of music and lyrical mantras. Over the centuries, it has become a cornerstone of Hindu religious practice and believers of religions such as Buddhism, Jainism, and Sikhism have also drawn upon its teachings.

In the modern world, many international authors have provided commentaries on Samveda. Notable contributors include the French philosopher Ernest Renan, the German scholar Georg Hüsing, and British South Asianist scholar Alan W. Entwistle. Each of these scholars offers a unique approach to interpreting the texts, exploring different aspects of their meaning and implications.

The presence of European commentary on Samveda began in 1875 when Ernest Renan published an essay entitled 'Essai sur le Samaveda.' In this essay, Renan argued that Samveda was more closely associated with music than with theology and also acknowledged the influence of European hymns on its composition. He believed that music was one of the most potent vehicles of religious expression and devoted much of his essay to examining how it shaped the Samveda.

Georg Hüsing, a noted German scholar, made the most significant contribution of the 19th century with his commentary on Samveda, Das Samveda (1920). He argued that Samveda should be seen as a holistic ancient text, one that is not simply a text of religious rhythms, but one that embraces many different aspects, including philosophy, theology, mythology, and aesthetic expression. He believed that Samveda was a form of musical chanting that represented the 'all-encompassing world-view' of ancient India.

Alan W. Entwistle was one of the first British South Asianists to provide a comprehensive and authoritative commentary on Samveda. His work, Samveda and Its Rituals (1958) sought to connect the text to the history and evolution of Indian ritual practices and religious expression. He argued that Samveda should be seen not just as a religious text but as a deep repository of cultural wisdom, containing teachings on moral values and ethical principle.

In conclusion, Samveda has been interpreted and commented on by a number of international authors over the years. Each of these scholars has contributed to our understanding of Samveda, providing valuable insight into the Vedic text from diverse points of view. By exploring the works of Ernst Renan, Georg Hüsing and Alan W. Entwistle, it is possible to gain a rich, global perspective on this ancient and mysterious spiritual text.

# CHAPTER THIRTEEN

# SAMAVEDA COMMENTARIES BY INDIAN SCHOLARS

The Samveda is one of the four primary scriptures of Hinduism, composed in the ancient Vedic language of Sanskrit. It is often viewed as the source of Vedantic philosophy and spirituality, forming an essential part of the Hindu tradition. Samveda consists of two parts: the Samhita, or the collection of hymns and mantras, and the Brahmana, or the commentary and explanatory passages.

The commentary on the Samaveda was written primarily by a group of scholars known as the Samaveda pandits, who used the ancient samhita text as the basis for their exposition. The earliest samhita commentaries date back to the tenth century, when the scholar and commentator, Shaunaka, authored his influential commentary on the text. His commentary is known as the Shaunakiya samhita and it is still utilized as an authoritative reference to the Samveda.

The scholar Yaska is another important contributor to the

Samvedic commentaries. His commentary, known as the Nirukta, is credited with helping to preserve the ancient language of Sanskrit and is often cited as the most important commentary on the Samveda. The Nirukta is also credited with introducing technical advances in the study of the Sanskrit language.

The controversial Valmiki also contributed to Samvedic commentaries, though his influence is most often felt in the post-Vedic Upanishadic literature. Valmiki's interpretation of the Samveda was heavily criticized by later scholars, but is still of great interest to scholars today, as it contains some interesting inconsistencies that can provide insight into the cultural context of the time.

The commentaries of the Samaveda were influential in preserving the language of Sanskrit and in helping to develop a culture of philosophical discourse in India. There is significant overlap between the commentaries and the overall philosophy of the Samveda, as the commentaries have helped to shape and direct the precise meanings of certain words and concepts, often providing a more detailed explanation of certain concepts. However, the commentaries have also been used as a tool for further interpretation, as the pandits often provided their own interpretations and interpretations of other scholars, contributing to the developing philosophical discourse of the Samaveda.

The Samaveda commentaries remain an integral part of Hinduism and are still studied and interpreted by modern scholars. The commentaries have proven to be an invaluable source of additional insight into the text and they provide a unique perspective on the philosophy and spirituality of the Samveda.

# CHAPTER FOURTEEN

# GEORG HUSING ABOUT SAMAVEDA

Georg Husing was a German philosopher who wrote a detailed treatise on the Samaveda. As one of the most important Vedic hymns, the Samaveda dates back to ancient India and was an important source of spiritual wisdom and guidance for Hindus centuries ago.

Georg Husing focused his essay primarily on the importance of the Samaveda in Hinduism, highlighting the spiritual and religious significance of it. He argued that the Samaveda served as the basis of Hinduism and provided the philosophical and metaphysical framework for Hindus to understand their religion.

Additionally, Husing noted that the Samaveda was incredibly influential in ritual practice, helping to inform many of the Vedic rites of religious prayer and meditation. He described these practices as a way of connecting to and experiencing God, as they enabled Hindus to immerse themselves and their minds into spiritual teachings that could not be found in any written text.

Husing also discussed the concept of "Tapas", a form of spiritual heat and energy in Hinduism which was believed to be difficult to attain but essential for spiritual growth and development. He argued that the chanting of Vedic hymns like the Samaveda was the best way to generate this Tapas in oneself, and that the reverberations of the words were powerful enough to open the minds and souls of those who chanted them, thus allowing them to gain a deeper understanding of their religion.

In conclusion, we can see that Georg Husing was a great admirer of the Samaveda, noting not just its religious importance, but also the spiritual benefits it could bring to individuals and the community more widely. The spiritual and philosophical grounds that Husing discussed in his essay have made the Samaveda an incredibly important part of the Hindu faith, and have enabled generations of Hindus to explore their innermost beliefs.

# CHAPTER FIFTEEN

# ERNEST RENAM
# ABOUT SAMAVEDA

Ernest Renan was one of the most influential authors of the 19<sup>th</sup> century whose academic works, including "History of the People of Israel", have been influential in the Jewish and Christian traditions. His works have helped to shape both academic and public discourse on Jewish identity, literature, and faith.

One of his most noteworthy works on Hinduism is "The Ancient History of the Samaveda". Renan wrote this work in the wake of his earlier works on the history of Jews and Christians. He believed that studying the Samaveda would reveal a new light on the ancient faith and culture of India and Hinduism.

In this work, Renan gave a detailed account of the Samaveda and its associated literature. At the outset, he established that the Samaveda is said to be the oldest of the four Vedas and is believed to be revealed scripture (śruti). The Samaveda, he argued, portrays the beliefs of an ancient Indian people who held a high degree of reverence for the recited Veda and the divinities present in the verses.

Renan further discussed the importance of the Samaveda in Hinduism by citing aspects of its literature, such as the significance of the sacrificial fire rituals, the reference to sacred places, and the invocation of Vedic gods. He also delved into the beliefs and values held by the ancient people associated with the Samaveda and their interpretation of the text.

Ernest Renan also discussed the works composed or inspired by the Samaveda. Renan argued that the body of Samavedic literature, including the Brahmanas, Aranyakas, and Upanishads, illuminated how Hindu beliefs evolved from the Samavedic period. He also discussed the various theories put forth by scholars about the authorship and style of these compositions and their implications.

Lastly, Renan explored how the Samaveda had helped to establish order in an otherwise chaotic world. Renan concluded the work by defending the Samaveda's importance in Hindu life and its role in the continuous transmission of Hindu traditions. In essence, Renan argued that the Samaveda not only preserved a unique cultural history, but it also served as a bridge between the generations and as a source of stability in a changing societal environment.

Ernest Renan's "History of the People of Israel" has had profound implications for shaping discourse on Jewish identity and faith. However, his work on the ancient Samaveda is equally important in understanding India's religious beliefs and culture. Through his vivid descriptions of the text, he revealed the dynamism underlying the Samaveda and its significance for Hinduism.

# CHAPTER SIXTEEN

# SHANKARACHARYA'S COMMENTARY ON SAMAVEDA

Shankaracharya's commentary on the Samaveda is a revered text among Hindu devotees. The Samaveda is one of the four primary Vedic texts and is an ancient collection of mantras, mainly used for chanting. The Samaveda, in particular, was renowned for its importance in liturgical chanting and Vedic rituals. Shankaracharya was one of the most famous sages of India who lived between 788 and 820 CE. His commentary on the Samaveda brings together the essence of traditional Vedic wisdom and his own interpretations of the text.

In his commentary on the Samaveda, Shankaracharya states that the core teachings of the Veda are that all life is intertwined and sacred. He professes that the hymns of the Samaveda should be chanted and understood in the spirit of unity, joy, and progress. Shankaracharya emphasizes that the chanting of the Samaveda produces divine energy, which can only be received if one understands its inner meaning. This divine energy is then used to fuel inner transformation, spiritual growth and further knowledge. Shankaracharya further claims that the Samaveda is a means to attaining Brahma. This is achieved through the understanding of the unity of life and the recognition of the inherent sacredness of all beings.

Shankaracharya also states that in order to experience the power of the Samaveda and its message of unity, a devotee must utilize both the heart and the intellect. He explains that the heart should be open to accept the truth of the message it is chanting, while the intellect should be used to comprehend its inner meanings. He prescribes independent and intensive study of the Samaveda as well as regular chanting of its hymns. This study and practice, according to Shankaracharya, is necessary to be able to gain immense spiritual power and eventually attain Brahma.

Shankaracharya's commentary on the Samaveda brings out the essence of Vedic philosophy in a profoundly beautiful and thought-provoking way. It encourages devotees to use both their heart and intellect to engage in its teachings, and provides a practical path to help individuals attain the heights of spiritual awakening. This commentary is still revered and revered today as one of the most important commentaries on the Vedic scriptures, and has helped many to gain insight into this ancient and profound wisdom.

# CHAPTER SEVENTEEN

# DAYANAND SARASWATI ON SAMAVEDA

Dayanand Saraswati, one of the greatest Indian reformers of the 19th century, was an avid scholar of the Vedas and the Samaveda. He founded the Hindu reform movement, the Arya Samaj, to promote the teachings of the Vedas and of the Samaveda. For Dayanand Saraswati, the Samaveda was of special importance as he believed it to be the most ancient parts of the Vedas. Dayanand Saraswati devoted much of his life to studying, translating and interpreting the Samaveda. He held the Samaveda in high regard, believing that its knowledge was essential to the preservation of Indian culture, practices and traditions.

Dayanand Saraswati saw the Samaveda as a source of divine knowledge and insight, but also as a way to improve the lives of all of humankind. He viewed the Samaveda as much more than an ancient religious text, but instead as a road map for all of humanity to inspire, guide and bring about change. In his book, Satyarth Prakash (Light of Truth), he wrote, "The Samaveda provides the knowledge necessary for spiritual improvement, the highest light for the supreme good of mankind". For him, the knowledge of the Samaveda was the key to spiritual liberation. He viewed its teachings as a way of removing greed, arrogance, social injustice and many other afflictions from the society.

He believed that the study of the Samaveda was the key to understanding the laws of dharma. He taught that these Vedic laws were the framework upon which a just and prosperous society could be built. He sought to restore the true meaning and value of the Samaveda and Vedic knowledge. His teachings were essential in the development of the Arya Samaj and its mission to restore the highest ideals and ideals of Hinduism and to promote understanding and harmony between all communities.

Dayanand Saraswati was confident that the knowledge of the Samaveda would increase the spiritual power and wisdom of ancient Vedic literature. He proclaimed, "We can thus understand that the yajnas and yagas of the Samaveda, if properly observed, provide ample opportunities of gaining perfect knowledge." This knowledge, he promised, would help bring about peace, prosperity and justice for all.

Dayanand Saraswati recognized the importance of keeping the Samaveda alive, and through his teaching efforts he sought to preserve its collective memory. For him, the Samaveda was an invaluable source of wisdom, not just for Hindus, but also for all humanity. His efforts to promote and preserve the Samaveda are a lasting testament to his untiring commitment to a world of greater spiritual and intellectual understanding.

# CHAPTER EIGHTEEN

# SAMVEDA AND VEDA VYAS

Veda Vyasa and Samaveda are two of the most important names in Hinduism and its related mythology. Not only is Veda Vyasa widely regarded as the author of the Mahabharata, one of the most widely read epics in India and around the world, but he is also attributed with arranging and editing the four Vedas, giving him a unique status in the pantheon of Hindu gods and goddesses. Meanwhile, the Samaveda is one of the four Vedas, making it an essential part of the Hindu faith.

Veda Vyasa, also known as Krishna Dvaipayan, is thought to be the author of several important texts in Hinduism, including the Mahabharata, Bhagavata Purana, Vedanta Sutras, and the Brahma Sutras. He is believed to have been born towards the end of the Dvapara Yuga, a period which it is claimed ended with the Mahabharata war. He is commonly portrayed with four arms, four faces, and four legs, and his parents are said to be Sage Parashara and the goddess Satyavati.

The Samaveda, meanwhile, is one of the four Vedas, with

Rishis compiling and reciting it. It is particularly known for the use of Samagana, the chanting of the Samaveda, which is believed to have a calming and spiritual effect on the listener. This veda includes mantras and hymns to be used in yajnas, sacrificial rituals considered essential as they help to reap spiritual rewards while making offerings to the gods.

The Samaveda also forms the basis for many Indian music traditions, with its hymns contributing to the development of Carnatic music. The notes in the hymns are known as svaras, and are used extensively in Indian music. Meanwhile, the Samaveda also includes one of the earliest explanations of musical scales, something which has been a cornerstone of Indian music since its inception.

Thus, Veda Vyasa and the Samaveda occupy a special place in Hinduism, with the former credited with arranging and editing the Vedas, and the latter being one of the four Vedas. Both names have lent their influence to aspects of modern Indian culture, such as its music and literature, making them important figures in India's cultural landscape.

# CHAPTER NINETEEN

# SUMMARY

The Samaveda is one of the four Vedas, the holiest and most ancient texts of Hinduism. It consists of chants and melodies used in Vedic worship. It consists primarily of hymns to the gods and provides sacred music for the sacrificial rituals of the priesthood, known as Brahmins. The Samaveda is also known as the Veda of chants or music, as it is the only Veda that is entirely devoted to music and song.

The Samaveda is composed of 1,549 stanzas, organized into eight books, or mandalas. These stanzas were composed in the pre-Vedic age, though the hymns were transmitted orally, from one generation to the next, until finally being written down, probably around 500 BC.

The Samaveda is an important source for Vedic culture, including the details of sacrificial rituals. It contains hymns to gods such as Indra, Agni and the Ashvins, as well as invocations to the three gods of prosperity, Susama, Dushkarma and Pushan. Successful completion of rites helped the gods to grant prosperity, health, strength and long life.

The Samaveda also includes hymns and songs for many special occasions, such as when the Vedic gods are to be celebrated, because the gods must be praised sweetly and regularly in order to receive their favor. It also contains songs sung to honor elders, and has numerous verses devoted to the praise of teachers, priests and theologians.

The Samaveda is also considered to be a source for Indian music and rhythmic composition. Although the Samaveda does not include detailed instructions for musical performance, the text does provide an ideal for performance: "Make your ears the audience and fill up the recitative with musical notes."

The Samaveda is a very important text in Hindu culture and history. It contains ancient chants and melodies to the gods, and instructions on how to perform rituals and worship. It serves as a source of inspiration for music and rhythmic composition, and still today plays a role in the lives of Hindus, who use it to invoke the gods and practice their ancient rituals.

# Author's Other Books

1. The Moments When I Met God
2. Kashiyile Theertha Pathangal
3. GURU GYAN VANI
4. Abhiprerak Gita
5. ASSI SE JAIN GHAT TAK
6. Hopelessness of Arjuna
7. The Soul and It's True Nature
8. Sense of Action (Karma)
9. Action through Wisdom
10. Action through Wisdom
11. THEORY AND PRACTICAL OF EVERY ACTION
12. LOGICAL UNDERSTANDING OF THE SUPREME
13. THE IMPERISHABLE SUPREME
14. Yatra Nishadraj se Hanuman Ghat Tak
15. Yatra Karnatak Ghat se Raja Ghat Tak
16. Yatra Pandey Ghat se Prayagraj Ghat Tak
17. Yatra Ranjendra Prasad Ghat se Dattatreya Ghat Tak
18. YaatraSindhiya Ghat se Gwaliar Ghat Tak
19. Yatra Mangala Gauri Ghat se Hanuman Gadhi Ghat Tak
20. Yatra Gaay Ghat Se Nishad Ghat Tak
21. MAA GANGA, GHATEN EVM UTSAV
22. Ganga Arti Dev Deepavali evam Any Utsav
23. Potentials of Digitalized India
24. VEDIC CONSCIOUSNESS
25. A Brief Introduction to Vedic Science
26. Kashi ke Barah Jyotirling
27. IMPACT OF MOTIVATION
28. Let's have a Milky Way Journey
29. Color Therapy in a Nutshell

30.  Rigveda in a Nutshell
31.  Yajurveda in a Nutshell
32.  Samveda in a Nutshell
33.  Atharva Veda in a Nutshell
34.  Ayurveda in a Nutshell
35.  Srimad Bhagavad Gita and Upanishad Connection

# Contact

DR. JAGADEESH PILLAI

PhD in Vedic Science

Four Times Guinness World Record Holder

Winner of Mahatma Gandhi Vishwa Shanti Puraskar and
Global Peace Ambassador

9839093003

myrichindia@gmail.com

drjagadeeshpillai@facebook

drjagadeeshpillai@instagram

jagadeeshpillai@youtube

www. JAGADEESHPILLAI.com

www.ingramcontent.com/pod-product-compliance
Lightning Source LLC
Chambersburg PA
CBHW031334130726
47988CB00007B/3130